Bushido

The Way
of the Samurai

BASED ON THE *HAGAKURE* BY

Tsunetomo Yamamoto

EDITED BY JUSTIN F. STONE
ORIGINAL TRANSLATION BY MINORU TANAKA

SQUAREONE
CLASSICS

Cover Designer: Phaedra Mastrocola
Typesetter: Gary A. Rosenberg
Series Consultant: Skip Whitson
Editor: Carola Roseby
Printer: Paragon Press, Honesdale, PA

Square One Publishers
Garden City Park, NY 11040
(516) 535-2010
www.squareonepublishers.com

Yamamoto, Tsunetomo, 1659–1719.
    [Hagakure. English]
    Bushido: the way of the samurai / translated by Minoru Tanaka;
edited by Justin F. Stone
        p. cm. — (Square One classics)
    ISBN 978-0-7570-0026-3 (pbk.)
    1. Bushido—Early works to 1800. I. Tanaka, Minoru, 1924 Jan. 3–
II. Stone, Justin F., 1916– III. Title. IV. Series
    BJ971.B8 Y3313 2001
    170'.44'09520903—dc21

                                                              2001003762

Square One Classics is an imprint of Square One Publishers, Inc.

Printed in Canada

10   9   8   7

Contents

BOOK TWO

BOOK THREE

BOOK NINE

BOOK TEN

BOOK ELEVEN

—◄o►—

Foreword

Minoru Tanaka speaks English better than anyone I have met in Japan. He has devoted himself, single-mindedly, to its study for many years, and now teaches the subject at a University near Osaka. At first I attempted to help him with his studies, but, when I found he was reading Chaucer and *Beowulf* in the original, I threw up my hands in despair and conceded I could no longer be of assistance to him.

So he is the proper person to have translated the classic *Hagakure*, I believe. As a rule, one translates from a foreign language to his own tongue. In this instance, Tanaka san has reversed the usual process. It is for this reason that I have stepped in, made some corrections, and occasionally rearranged the wording of his excellent translation. Some of the ideas in the book are so startling that it has not been easy to put them into workable English. Where possible, we have left unchanged the quaint and colorful expressions found in the original, rather than prosaically reducing them to everyday English.

I first met Tanaka sensei in Kyoto in 1969. I was ambling down a side street off Kurasama Doori, on my way to the alley where the main entrance of the Tenrikyo Church community at which I was staying was located, when I heard a loudspeaker announce that English class was about to begin. Noticing that I was passing a small junior college, I spontaneously turned in the entrance and followed some students to the class. It turned out that Tanaka was teaching it, and we quickly became good friends. I casually invited him to visit me at the Church, and he did so a few days later at exactly the time we were about to have formal tea ceremony for three charming female interpreters from Geneva. Tanaka joined us for what he sheepishly admitted was his first chanoyu (tea ceremony). Subsequently, he came to visit me every Saturday, at which time we would drink tea while he helped me with my Japanese and I attempted to aid him with his excellent English. Years later he visited me in America, and we worked together to bring the *Hagakure* to the English-speaking public. All because of a well-timed loudspeaker announcement!

It is my belief that it is important for Westerners to understand the seemingly strange concepts of Bushido, not only as a guide to events of the past, but as a primer for understanding the Japanese business mentality of today.

It is hard for Westerners to believe that Japanese employees will not take vacations because of loyalty to their employers. Such loyalty to the large corporation borders on the fanatic, and it is a common occurrence to hear poorly paid subordinates joyfully sing company songs and chant slogans before work begins each day. This is not done cynically. The employer occupies a paternalistic position in relation to his employees. Seldom is anyone fired. In the case of an outright bungling, or even dishonesty, a face-saving excuse may be fabricated and the offending one transferred to another position. And employees, even highest executives, do not quit their jobs or look for better-paying opportunities. Employment is usually of the lifetime variety, with the employer (just as with the Lord, in Medieval times) taking a deep interest in the employee's personal life, family, children, etc. One may rightly say the vice-presidents of today are the loyal Samurai retainers of the Clan (in this case, the Corporation), who will give themselves unstintingly for the common, not the personal, cause. It is partially because of this two-sided loyalty and the strength it imparts that Japan rose from a bombed out, defeated nation to a position of envied affluence in less than thirty years. This way of thinking is completely contrary to what we know in the West, and I believe Tanaka's translation will enable many Westerners to better understand what they are competing against.

It will be interesting to the reader to note the many Zen Buddhist terms that are used in this book. Facing death every day, the Samurai warriors had to go beyond life and death in order to live with courage and equanimity, and the practical teaching and practice of Zen enabled them to do so. Royalty was attracted to Shingon Buddhism, with its ritual and trappings; the philosophically minded gravitated to Tendai; and the common person naturally followed the way of devotion, Shin Buddhism. But the Samurai, not interested in words and speculations, found the meditation and twenty-four-hour awareness of Zen invaluable in his calling as "Warrior-Knight" and made full use of it.

It is necessary for the reader to abstain from judging while reading this sometimes strange book. I suggest it be read as the important document it is, without praise or condemnation (the praise probably coming from those involved in the Martial Arts and similar groups).

There is little reason to doubt that *Hagakure* will play an important role in the future of Japan, as it has in the past, and our leaders had better learn to comprehend it.

If there is any awkwardness of language, please put the blame on me. I have been loath to needlessly tamper with the native mode of expression.

Justin Stone
Albuquerque, New Mexico

Historical Overview

The Shogunate Rule (1603–1867) was a period of peace and political stability. In order to preserve its power, the Shogunate Government maintained a closed-door policy toward all foreign countries. Under the Shogunate system, each clan was relatively independent but was required to pay allegiance to the central government of Shogunate. Within each clan, the lord and his samurais composed the leading class. As a ruling group, they held dominion over the farmers, manufacturers, merchants, and craftsmen.

The author of *Hagakure*, Tsunetomo Yamamoto (1659–1719), was a member of the powerful Nabeshima clan. As a youth, Yamamoto attended on his master, Lord Mitsushige Nabeshima. For thirty years, Yamamoto devoted his life to the service of his Lord and clan. His service varied from being a page boy to a highly respected samurai. Then, on the death of Mitsushige Nabeshima in 1700, Yamamoto renounced the world and retired to a hermitage in the mountains. Ten years later, Tsuramoto Tashiro visited him and became his close friend and disciple. For a period of seven years (1710–1716), they lived together in the mountain retreat. During this time, Tashiro recorded verbatim what his master said to him at random.

Yamamoto forbade Tashiro to publish the talks that were later to be called *Hagakure* (which literally means "Hidden Behind the Leaves.") The reason he forbade publication was that he knew his teachings were too radical and excessive for the then-peaceful world. Also, his ideas were not altogether consistent with the then-prevalent official study of the teachings of Confucius (who advocated peace and order).

During the period that *Hagakure* was being recorded, peace within the country enabled the people to devote time to cultural matters. Even the samurais, who were expected to be warriors, tended to forget their experiences in the Civil Wars (1467–1568). They began to neglect their military practices and their mastery of Bushido, the Way of the Samurai, and gave more and more of their time and attention to personal accomplishments rather than to the military arts and the traditional loyal service of their Lord. They did this knowing that they were expected to be efficient bureaucrats in the service of the Lord and clan, and, as a result, tended to become tender and effeminate. They began to act out of their own self-interests. No definite ideal prevailed among the samurais at this time.

During this period, Yamamoto came to the conclusion that respectability and discretion were based on Man's preference of life to death. In other words, he saw cowardice and fear as the basis for all the various kinds of humanitarian ideas and philosophies. Regardless of ideas and philosophies, he suggested that the samurai throw away all self-imposed limitations caused by the choice of life rather than death. In his talks, he wanted every samurai to become a super-man. But he wanted super-men who were capable of gaining great power, not for their own self-interest, but for the interest of the clan. He wanted super-men who were capable of operating effectively for the solidarity of the clan.

In spite of Yamamoto's prohibition, the original writings of *Hagakure* were secretly copied by hand. They were then circulated among the so-called "awakened" samurais. Yet, the book was kept secret from the general public until it was eventually published in 1906. The publication influenced many Japanese—particularly generals and officers and others engaged in the control of military power.

The eighty years or so from the Restoration of Imperial Rule in 1867 to the surrender of Japan to the Allied Forces in 1945 was a period of continual warfare for Japan. This warfare was based upon the economic development and military expansion of the country. During this period, the relation between the Lord and his samurais changed into a similar relation between the Emperor and his trusted soldiers. During the last stage of the Pacific War (1941–1945), the *Kamikaze* fighting pilots—made up mostly of students—rationalized their action of self-sacrifice through the often quoted passage of *Hagakure:*

"I have found the essence of Bushido: to die!"

When the Empire of Japan surrendered to the Allied Powers in 1945, *Hagakure* was "burned" because it was considered to be an ideological war criminal. Though the book was "burned," its spirit still survived. It is the energy from this spirit that has enabled the Japanese people to revive and rapidly develop their economy and national prestige.

Today there exists a general belief that a powerful force—militarism based upon the so-called economic imperialism—is again reviving in Japan. The very existence of this belief—be it valid or not—accounts for the recent revival of *Hagakure* among the Japanese people. Since the end of the Pacific War, four different editions of *Hagakure* have been published in Japan. There is no doubt that *Hagakure* has come to be read by more and more Japanese as a book of today. Indeed, one of the latest editions has emphasized the up-to-dateness of *Hagakure* as a book showing how individual members of an organization should cooperate with one another in a common cause. According to this edition, the basic pattern of the Japanese society has remained the same: The present "clans" take the form of the Japanese business company. The executive of the company, or often the company itself, is the "Lord." The businessmen are the present-day "samurais," who literally give themselves to their "clans."

Hagakure is a book for those interested in discovering the truth about Japan and the Japanese people. It will certainly give the reader a deeper insight into the traditional Japanese mentality.

Minoru Tanaka
Osaka, Japan

Hagakure

by
Tsunetomo Yamamoto

Transcriber's Preface

These eleven volumes from beginning to end must be burned in due course of time. I have put down verbatim what the author remembers for (his own) future reference: on the society; the right and wrong of samurais; conjecture; manners and customs, etc.

These notes may very well arouse ill-feeling. It is best to remember that the author has repeatedly and strictly told me to burn these manuscripts.

We first met March 5th in the year of Hoei (1710).

> How far from the floating world
> these mountain cherries are!
> —Tsunetomo Yamamoto

> Under a white cloud
> I have just come across a flower.
> —Tsuramoto Tashiro

(The above are haiku poems composed when the author and transcriber met each other for the first time.)

Author's Introduction

A Quiet Talk by Night

As a retainer to this Nabeshima clan, you must devote yourself toward the studies of your own country.[1] But now, the need for this study has dropped from the eye of every samurai.

The general drift of clan studies is to trace the history of a particular clan back to its foundation. By following the general drift, we can credit the present prosperity of our household to its founders: To the benevolent and courageous mind of Gochyu;[2] To the deeds and faith of Riso.[3] For, by their virtue appeared (was born) Takanobu[4] and Nippo Nabeshima.[5] Due to their power and authority, our clan has been prosperous and secure, and it has had no equal up to the present time.

The samurais of this clan have completely forgotten to uphold this kind of cause. Instead, they value Buddhas belonging to other places. I, for my own part, am quite dissatisfied with this fact, since Confucius, Buddha, Kusunaki,[6] and Shingen[7] have never served our clan. It is needless to say that their teachings must inevitably fall short of the manners and customs of our own tradition.

Both at the time of plain clothes (peace) and the time of helmets and armor (war), it is sufficient for both high and low to revere the founders and their offspring so we can learn from their examples. Then we (present samurais of the clan) will be able to manage everything without fail.

As people are supposed to revere their respective idols and their principal images in their own way,[8] then, as far as serving the Nabeshima clan is concerned, there is no need to learn any other branch of knowledge (other than the studies of our clan) at any other place.

Once you have mastered the practices and habits of our own clan, you may learn other ways as a pastime, for your own amusement. But, when you come to think of it, there is not a problem that cannot be solved with the help of this knowledge (of our own clan).

Those who neglect this study of our own country would not be able to give a word of reply to such questions (asked) by members of other clans, as: "What is the history of the Nabeshima clan?" or, "How was your clan established?" or, "You have been reputed to be the best spear-thrusters (warrior-samurais) in Japan; but what are the details of your distinguished military service?"

The duty of each member who serves this house is none other than that he should carry out his respective, official responsibility. However, most of the members, on the contrary, may find pleasure in other topics and dislike their own office. Consequently, they put the cart before the horse and blunder grossly.

The good examples of service are Nippo and Katsushige, the first Lord. During their time (of rule), each subject applied himself to performing his own duty. From the high, they sought for useful subjects; from the low, the samurais were eager to be of service. In this manner, the minds of the Lords and those of the samurais were connected; for this reason, the power of the household was cumulative and grew great.

The efforts, pains, and labor on the part of Nippo were too much to tell. He cut a bloody trail and frequently made himself ready for harakiri.[9] But, by some wondrous chance, he finally succeeded in making his household stand on its own.

Likewise, Katsushige (later the first Lord) met with an occasion in which he came very close to harakiri; but he finally became the first Lord. He, in person, took the lead in the working of bow and arrow; the rule of the samurais in the house; the government of the country; and the administration of strategy points (fortresses). He even organized miscellaneous duties. He firmly believed in Buddha and the gods. After his retirement, he sat among wastepaper for the rest of his life and wrote a book. He said, "If I think little of the household that Nippo established, it would be quite irresponsible of me. I must take care that it goes on prosperously for the generations to come.

"Now that the time is peaceful and quiet, our society is

on its way to becoming luxurious; it is unprepared for the ways of bow and arrow; it is becoming proud. Accordingly, there arise many blunders: the high and the low both get hard up, and this is a discredit to the clan both within and without. These kinds of blunders will undermine and over-throw the house.

"The veteran samurais have died out. The youth follow the trend of this day alone. So, if I could hand down something in writing, perhaps they might learn the tradition and the spirit of this clan by referring to the book."

Of course, the book was intended to be a secret one. But I (i.e., the author of *Hagakure*) have heard elders speak about this book. The rumor is that it is a book on tactics called *Kachikuchi (The Key to Victory)* and it was orally passed on at the time of inheritance.

It is also said that two other books, *Shichokakuchisho* and *Senkosan'iki* [10] were handed down, firsthand.

Katsushige also made notes on the following: on the customs of the house and on the disposition of affairs with the Shogunate (central government). He also made detailed rules about home administration. Boundless efforts they were! By his merits, the house can enjoy today's security and everything looks quite auspicious.

Therefore, and this may sound very disrespectful, the present Lord (the fourth Lord, Yoshishige), by reminding himself of the endeavors and pains of the founder, Naoshige, and the first Lord, Katsushige, and also, by at least perusing the writings he inherited, would do well to strengthen his resolution to govern the state earnestly.

Since he has been flattered and indulged as a young Lord (successor) and has experienced no hardship and trials and has no knowledge of his own clan, and tends to have his own way in everything and neglects his own duty (as a Lord), a lot of unnecessary reformations have taken place in the last few years. The establishment of the clan has been weakened. Taking advantage of this situation, shrewd and smart people with competitive minds, but without experience, have devised many ideas so as to insinuate themselves into the favor of the Lord, ideas whereby they act important and do what they like arbitrarily and make a mess of things. Here are some examples of the mess they have created: strife between the three branch families; establishment of new offices next in rank to the Chief Retainer's;[11] employment of members of other clans; changes in the organization of the reserve samurais; exchange of residences; newly appointed elders corresponding in rank to the relatives of the Lord's family; the demolition of the villa, Koyoken, that Lord Katsushige constructed; revision of the criminal code; rearrangement of the status of shrines and temples; building of a new villa; reckless change in the formation of light-legged soldiers; arrangement and disposition of equipment; the destruction of the west villa, etc.

Every item is a failure as a result of the Lord's attempt to bring these new-fangled matters into effect. But, thanks to the firm establishment on the part of the founders, no instance of misrule has ever shaken the foundation (of our clan).

If only both the high and the low remain faithful to the

directions of Lord Naoshige and Katsushige, the clan will be strongly and peacefully organized and governed in such a way that every member feels content, no matter how clumsily affairs may be carried on.

There has not been a foolish Lord in the clan, nor an evil Lord. And each has been counted as one of the best Lords in Japan. This is a miraculously fortunate family, thanks to the faith of each Lord.

No samurai has ever been driven out of this land; no outsiders have ever been accepted (or employed). Even if they (our samurais) did ronin,[12] they were allowed to stay within the territory. And the sons and grandsons of samurais who were told to do harakiri were also allowed residence in this land.

Since you are born through some wondrous chance into the clan in which benevolence and loyalty are very deep, everyone—to say nothing of the farmers and merchants—is greatly indebted to the clan beyond any verbal description.

In view of this fact, be firmly resolved to offer yourself in your service so that you can make up for the favor (privilege) of being a member of this clan. And if the Lord patronizes you, prove yourself useful by throwing away your self-mind. Even if you are ordered to do either ronin or harakiri, take it as a form of service and convince yourself that you shall inevitably die and be born again out of the depths of the mountains or from under the ground only in order to work for the clan. This is the first requirement of the Nabeshima samurais and the pith and marrow of us.

It is indeed inadequate for a monk [*bonze*], which I now

am, to say that I have never looked forward to Nirvana.[13] Only it is deeply engrained in my liver that I should be born again into this Nabeshima clan every time I have another incarnation so that I can do service to this clan.

For Nabeshima samurais, no spirit and no talent is necessary so long as you have the ambition to shoulder the whole clan by yourself, so to speak, to carry the burden alone, if necessary.

Can any individual be inferior to another individual? You cannot carry out your mastery (of service) if you are not proud. Your mastery will not bear fruit if you don't go about with the intention of securing the house on your own.

Perhaps, like hot water in a kettle, your resolution may become cooler. There is a way to keep it hot. Our unique vows are:

1. Never lag behind in the practice of Bushido.

2. Always be loyal and devoted in the service to your Lord.

3. Do your duty to your parents.

4. Stir up your compassion for all sentient beings in order to devote yourself to the service of others.

These are the keys. Recite these four vows while praying to the gods and Buddha. Then you will not run backwards, but you will be able to double your power and energy. You will go ahead inch by inch like a measuring worm. Even the Buddha and the gods decided on vows before they initiated their pursuits.

BOOK ONE

The Essence of Bushido

I have found the essence of Bushido: to die! In other words, when you have a choice between life and death, then always choose death: this is all that you must remember. It is neither troublesome nor difficult. You have only to go on with a clenched stomach. Any other ideas are unnecessary and futile.

"If you die before you hit your target, then it will be the death of a dog." If you say this, then your attitude is the Kamigata of Bushido. It is a very vain and calculating attitude at its best.

But if you are forced, then it is impossible for you to make the right choice between life and death. It goes without saying that every person would prefer to live rather than to die. Accordingly, people will try to rationalize for the choice of life. If you make the choice of life and do not hit the target, you will be called a coward. Before you make the choice, realize what a critical position you are in. On the other hand, if you but make the choice of death and fail to hit the target, your body will eventually die but no shame will come to you. No shame will come to you even though you will be regarded as crazy and as dying like a dog.

This is the essence of Bushido. In order to master this essence, you must die anew, every morning and every night. If you continually preserve the state of death in everyday life, you will understand the essence of Bushido, and you will gain freedom in Bushido. Then you will be able to fulfill your duty to the offices of the household of the Lord without a mistake and for the rest of your life.

Two Ways of Thinking

There are some who can spontaneously come up with good ideas; this is done through natural gift. There are others who can form ideas only after pillow-breaking speculation in bed. There is a difference in speed according to individual natures. But if you refer to the four vows (in the introductory essay) and think freely from your own personal interest, then miraculously good ideas will occur to you.

We take it for granted that effective, problem-solving thinking requires deep thought. This is not necessarily true. The truth is, if you base your thinking upon your selfish desires, the working of your mind is reduced to the working of a malicious intellect. No wonder your ideas end up as being selfish and evil.

It is usual for the fool not to be able to transcend thinking based on "I." But after all, in the face of a big problem, you cannot be wide of the mark if you only set aside "I" and then press the four vows upon your heart.

Two Methods of Criticism

It is of utmost importance to admonish others with the intention of helping them overcome their faults. It is an act of compassion and the first requirement of your service. The way of advising others must be carried out with utmost care and caution. It is quite easy to see good and evil in others. It is equally as easy to criticize others. Most people think it is an act of kindness to say what others do not like or hesitate to hear. But they give up if their advice is not accepted; they stop here, but this is quite ineffective. The result is that they put others to shame, which is the same as abuse or insult. They speak only to relieve their own hearts.

In giving advice, you must recognize whether the other person is inclined to accept it or not. You must begin by getting on intimate terms with him; you must do this to the extent that he places his confidence in you, and you in him. Then he can put his trust in your words. Attract his attention by way of common interests. Devise appropriate ways of speaking and know the right season (time) to speak. Make the most of personal correspondence. Insinuate your point into the words you deliver at the time of farewell. Refer to your own weakness and failures. You would do well to let him discover your point without directly mentioning his weakness. First praise his merits or strong points and cheer up his mood. Devise means to bring about the circumstances in which he will accept your implied or intended advice. In other words, if you make him feel thirsty, he will want to drink. This way of admonition is advice in the true sense of the word. It is exceptionally difficult to practice.

Through my own experience, I have also learned that many faults and weakness have been so ingrained that it is not possible to break out of these bad habits by ordinary efforts.

It is quite in keeping with compassion that colleagues should unite together in the common cause of service. Then they can admonish each other from their own point of view. This should be done on a confidential basis. When all colleagues put their "souls" together and correct each other's disgressions, this leads to an act of compassion for all sentient beings.

How can you reform others if you disgrace them?

How to Stop Yawning

It is rude to yawn in the faces of other people. If by chance you begin to yawn, stroke your forehead and then your yawn should stop. If this does not work, then lap your lips with the tongue without opening your mouth. Or you might yawn behind your sleeve or apply your hand to your mouth so as to hide the yawning from view.

This is also true of sneezing, which makes you look silly and foolish.

Foresight in Relationships

On the previous night, make your plans for the next day and write them down. This is the method of disposing of affairs in advance of others.

Before making a visit, one should make inquiries about everything concerning the other party. Also, one should make a mental note of the ways of greeting and the topics of conversation.

When you are told to accompany the Lord, or when you visit others yourself for a talk, consider the character of the host before you begin. This is the way to bring about compatibility and good manners.

If you attend an exclusive samurai's party and feel timid, you cannot do your part in making it a successful party. You had first better prepare by convincing yourself that you will have a grand time. And you should feel grateful for the invitation.

At any rate, apart from business, you'd better not go where you are not invited. If you are invited, play the part of the finest guest. This is the thing! Come up with the previously calculated image of the party. To know what manners to use is most important.

You also have to choose the right time to leave. Leave before you bore others, but don't leave too early.

When you take part in a feast, don't be too modest about the food; this will displease the host. After saying "no thank you" once or twice, accept what is offered. This is the case when you pay a casual visit and are detained.

Samurais of Satori and Non-Satori

Samurais of satori and non-satori are referred to in a book on tactics. The former is one who, after going through a crisis, makes the most of his experience; he is also the one who can use his forethought to quickly settle problems in case of an emergency. Accordingly, we call samurais of satori those who can come to conclusions before meeting tens of thousands of matters.

Non-satori samurais might be able to come up with a make-shift solution, but this is achieved merely through good luck.

Those who do not scrutinize everything before the events occur may justly be called samurais of non-satori.

If the Water Is Clear No Fish Will Live

I hear that some samurai is preaching thrift. He is fussy and fastidious and feminine with his preaching. This is not desirable.

It sometimes happens that, if the water is too clear, then the fish will no longer dwell there. When there are algae and water plants, fish can safely grow by hiding behind the plants. As long as people overlook matters, then inferiors can, without any fear, lead an easy and peaceful life.

You must know this as far as your personal conduct is concerned.

The Marrow of Service

Looking at today's samurais, they are all keeping their eyes on lower objectives. Their eyes are like the eyes of pickpockets. For the most part, they strive for their own mercenary aims or they merely display their cunning shrewdness; or, when it comes to those apparently self-composed samurais, they are just posers.

In order to deserve the name of samurai, you must offer your life to the service of your Lord. You must become a ghost after the completion of a frenzied death. You must always keep the Lord's affairs in mind. You also must report to the Lord about affairs that you have arranged. Then you can help to lay a firm foundation for the state.

There is no difference in the amount of service between high and low. So you ought to sit tightly on this understanding.

You must prepare yourself not to digress from this practice of constant service even if you are exhorted to do so by the oracles of the gods or of the Buddha.

The Use of Onlookers

While disliking injustice, it is very difficult to carry out acts of justice. Also, more mistakes arise if you think that to adhere to justice is always the best way. There is a higher way than mere justice. Indeed, it is difficult to find this way. We may call this way "the use of a higher, wiser intellect." Seen through this higher, wiser intellect, justice looks thinner and without much substance. Yet, you cannot attain this higher wisdom until you personally learn it through your own experience. But, if you cannot come across this way, there is a method to obtain this higher wisdom: to consult with others.

Even those who themselves have not achieved this way can still look at others' affairs from the side, objectively.

Thus people say "onlookers see more than players." They say you must find your own faults through speculation. But the best way, of course, is to consult others. To listen to others talk and to read books is necessary in order to keep close to the learning of the previous generation.

You must throw away your own judgment.

High Upon High

An old, retired swordsman once said, "There are levels in the course of mastery throughout your life. At the lowest level of skill and ability, one thinks of himself and others as poor. He thinks this because he has mastered only a little. Needless to say, a person at this level is not at all useful.

"At the middle level, one is still useless, but he can at least understand that he and others have mastered only a little.

"At a high level, since a person has made something his

own, he is proud of his accomplishment. And he is also glad of the praise of others. He grieves over the shortcomings of others. This kind of person is at least useful."

At a higher level, one pretends to know nothing, yet others understand that he holds an upper hand. The majority of people cannot get beyond this level.

Beyond this higher level, there is one further step: the level of the trackless road. If you travel deeper into the trackless road, infinite secrets will finally appear. Then you can never see the end of your mastery. Then you truly realize how lacking you are. You have only to go ahead with your intention of mastery in mind. You go forward without pride and without humility.

Yagyu (a swordsman who taught the Shogun himself) once said, "I know nothing about how to win over others. I only know the way to win over myself."

Your life is something you build every day. You must convince yourself that you have surpassed yesterday. And tomorrow you must feel that you have surpassed today. In this way there is no end to your mastery.

Think Lightly
on Serious Matters

A note by Naoshige reads, "Think of serious matters in a light manner." A footnote to this item by Ittei Ishida (a scholar attached to the Nabeshima clan) is as follows: "Think of trifles in an earnest and thoughtful way."

There are only a few considerations that are serious for you. You can make your decision about these few serious matters beforehand in ordinary circumstances. Accordingly, you previously think about these serious matters and then you have only to take out the previously arrived at conclusions when you need them. On the other hand, if you are not prepared, then it will be difficult to think lightly of grave matters when you meet with occasions on which you have to make an instant decision. At such a time you will be unable to hit the mark.

Therefore, to make your own ground firm is the basis for making your decisions.

The above is the basis of the saying "Think of grave matters in a light fashion."

People You Can Trust

At an official inquiry about a certain samurai's advancement, it was about to be decided that he should not be promoted because he had been an alcoholic.

Before the decision was made, someone spoke up, "If you abandon those who have made blunders, you cannot hope to make great people out of them. And since they are sorry for their failures, they will try to make up for them. So they will prove more useful later on. Therefore, this man must be promoted."

Another samurai asked, "Do you sponsor him?"

"Of course I do," was the reply.

Everyone asked, "On what grounds do you sponsor him?"

"I sponsor him because he is one who once made a mistake. Those who have never made a mistake are in danger."

Eventually, the samurai was promoted to a higher post.

The Thinking Process

It is not good to keep your own house. After exerting a make-shift effort, it is a mistake to look wise on the level of a definite conclusion. First try to get hold of a seed of thought firmly and see to it that the seed will ripen to bear fruit; all your life, you must never stop. Yet it is out of the question to think of any one thought or pattern of thought that you have come across as coming up to the final level. You must try to reject every way as unsatisfactory. You must go on with your mastery; you must seek, as long as you live, to attain the right way. You must keep your mind from resting easy. Within such efforts is hidden the right way itself.

Models to Imitate

Ittei Ishida, a clan scholar, once remarked, "Even a bad calligraphy (handwriting) will be fairly improved if a good model is used for imitation."

This is true of servants, too. If you follow after good servants, you will naturally become a good one, too. But it is true that today there is not a good servant to model after.

Since there is no individual who is perfect all by himself, you had better take one good, strong point from each person to use as your model. In other words, you decide to learn good manners from A; courage from B; oratory from C; good conduct from D; integrity from E; quick determination from F; etc. In this way, you can construct one good model out of individual merits.

As far as the tens of thousands of arts are concerned, students tend to imitate their master's weak points rather than his strong points. This is useless. There may be a person who has good manners but lacks honesty. You are likely to imitate and learn the lack of honesty and pay no attention to his good manners.

If your eye is able enough to see good qualities in others who are apparently inferior to you, then they can be your masters, even though they have their shortcomings as well.

The Puppet Show World

The Japanese word is "maboroshi," which means "vision" or "dream-like state." In India, they name masters of magic as vision-creators. In the world, everything is like a puppet. Therefore, we use "maboroshi."

Conduct at the Wine Feast

A great many samurais fall into disgrace due to heavy drinking. A thousand pities!

First measure your capacity, and keep yourself in check. But you may sometimes find yourself drinking too much. Above all, be on guard all the while that you are imbibing wine. Keep yourself prepared to cope with the settlement of unexpected accidents. Remember that the wine feast is a matter of the public world. There are too many eyes present at the feast. You must be cautious.

The Use of the High Spirit

When you go to look after one who has suffered misfortune, one word is of utmost importance because your inner person may be known by that single word.

At all events, samurais are not good when they are worn and dispirited. Samurais are useless unless they have the spirit to rise above the sea (of troubles and difficulties). This spirit can encourage other samurais.

Lesson From the Heavy Rain

Here is my lesson from the heavy rain: on your way, you meet a shower. You dislike to get wet, so you hurry along the streets running under the eaves. Still, you get wet all the same. As long as you accept that you will get wet, you won't suffer from being wet.

The Winner's Spirit

In his old age, Tetsuzan said, "I thought that grappling (ju-jitsu, now judo) is different from Sumo in that to win you have only to lie on the opponent, even though you suffer under him in the middle (i.e., in the midst of battle, your opponent may be on top of you). But recently, I've come to know that, if someone draws us apart when I am under my opponent, then it is I who will be judged the loser. To win at first, therefore, is to win all the time."

Bringing Up Samurai Children

Here is the particular way to bring up samurai children: first inspire them with courage, even when they are very small. You must never scare them nor deceive them, even in a joke. If they contract cowardice while young, the cowardice will last the whole life. Hence cowardice will become their life-long fault.

Careless parents may allow their children to become frightened by thunder and lightning. They may tell their children not to go into the dark. They may tell their children horrible stories to stop them from crying.

If you would scold your children too severely when they are too young, they will grow up to be timid. Also, you must not let them fall into bad habits that you will not be able to mend by scolding them.

You must direct them so that they learn by themselves

the proper way of speaking and the mastery of good manners. You had better keep them from learning avarice and greed. The rest is up to you. If they have the same gifts as other children, then their defects can be corrected.

Children of quarreling couples are said to neglect their duty to their parents. And this is not surprising; after all, even the young birds and beasts are infected by the things they see and hear from their parents.

Some foolish mothers bring about family conflict between the father and the children. It seems that these mothers become excessively fond of their children. Should the father admonish the children, then the mother, out of mistaken love, takes sides with the children. Then the children and the father are at odds with each other. It would appear that, out of base feelings, this kind of mother draws close to her sons and depends upon them for her old-age security.

Arts and Crafts

It might only be said of the samurais of other clans that the arts and crafts will help the body. As far as samurais of our clan are concerned, arts and crafts destroy the body. Those who are skilled in even a single art (*gei*) are to be termed as geisha, not samurai. You must be regarded by others as samurai and not geisha. It is not until you have realized that arts and crafts of any kind are harmful to samurai that you can make the most of the skills and abilities you thereby acquire. You must keep this fact in mind.

Groundless Suffering

A samurai once said, "Samurais fear becoming ronin because it involves thousands of troubles and miseries. So they become very depressed when they are told to do ronin. But once you actually do ronin, you will not find it as difficult as you expected; quite different from your fearful anticipation. I personally want to do ronin again."

He is quite right. As for the way of death, if you previously learn how to die, you can die with ease of mind.

Since disaster is not as terrible as your unnecessary anxiety would have you expect, it is absurd to suffer distress in advance. This distress is caused by overactive imagination.

You must understand, at all times, that the end for all samurais is either ronin or harakiri.

Testing Your Friend's Loyalty

It is said that if you want to see the true mind of your friend, then you should get sick. While keeping company in usual circumstances, if your apparent friend stands off from you in sickness or in other troubles, then he can best be called a coward. After all, it is a true samurai who keeps on intimate terms with his colleagues, especially when they are unhappy. He presents gifts and donations; he looks after his friends.

Of those who once helped you, you must not drift apart from them throughout your life. It is in these unfortunate circumstances that your friend's sincerity is made clear.

Normally, most people can rely on you when they are in trouble. But they will never even think of you once they are out of their trouble.

Good and Evil

You cannot judge whether one is good or evil by noting whether he is prosperous or not. Rise and fall is a matter of the Way of Heaven. Good and evil is the Way of Man. But, for morality's sake, we attribute prosperity and decline to good and bad respectively.

Discharging Servants

My father used to give leave to his servants at the end of the year, although he was aware that they had made blunders earlier than that. Thus he allowed them to save face and prevented the possibility of their carrying a grudge against him.

On the Men of Learning

The calculating samurais must inevitably turn into cowards. Their calculation deals with whether they can gain profit or suffer loss. They cannot stop constantly referring to the idea of loss and gain. They think of death as loss and life as gain. No wonder they dislike death. That is why they become cowards. And the men of learning hide their cowardice behind the screen of their intellect and oratory eloquence. People tend to misjudge them.

Burn With Mad Death

Naoshige once said, "The Bushido signifies desperate death. Several tens of sane samurais could not kill a single samurai (who burns with this mad death)."

Sane men of calmly composed mind cannot accomplish a great enterprise. You have only to get wildly crazy to the point of death. The moment discretion and consideration mingle with your Bushido, you will surely hesitate and lag behind in your enterprise.

To the Bushido, loyalty and filial duty will naturally follow from your madness. Because in this desperate death, both of these qualities dwell in your actions.

The Samurai Superintendent Officer

A superintendent officer is lax if he does not have a bird's-eye view of the whole situation. The reason the office of the superintendent officer has been established is that it will help the Lord to govern the nation. It is impossible for a Lord alone to keep an eye on every nook and corner. But, by means of a superintendent officer, the Lord can understand his own conduct. He can understand the vice and good deeds of the Chief Retainer. He can understand the success and failure of the administration. He can understand the public opinion. And he can understand the pains and pleasures of the lower masses. From this knowledge, the Lord can reform his own way of ruling.

It is the role and responsibility of a superintendent officer to watch higher people. But, on the other hand, when he gets wind of and finds out the wicked deeds of the lower masses and reports them to the Lord, then there arises no end of evil. This is quite contrary to the intended purpose of a superintendent officer. The straight (people) are rare among the lower masses. But their evil deeds will not go so far as to harm the state.

Investigators should investigate the suspects in such a way that their excuses can be proven true; this is so that they may be acquitted. This is ultimately for the good of the state.

Passing the First Barrier

(On a low level,) it is still unsatisfactory if you remain unfrightened when you find yourself face to face with disaster and difficulties. (On a higher level,) you ought to go through troubles with courage and elation. This means you have passed the first barrier. This is another way of saying that, if the water rises, the ship rises, too.

"My Master Is Human And So Am I"

(A Japanese proverb)

On hearing and seeing the master, it is very spiritless of you to think you cannot reach him. First, think of yourself and your master as both human beings. Then also think, "In what way can one human be inferior to another human?" So thinking, you can hope to reach him. Then you have already entered the way.

"It is not because Confucius had tried to master the way, but it is because he had set his heart on learning at the age of fifteen that he became a saint," says the scholar of the clan, Ittei Ishida. In other words, you can have correct satori the moment you have set a definite aim in your life for the first time, as one of the Buddhist scriptures says.

Making Important Decisions

One of our ancestors said, "Consider as you breathe seven times."

Lord Takanobu remarked, "Long thought results in dull and commonplace conclusions."

Also Lord Naoshige observed, "Seven out of ten things that you don't feel like doing will end up as failures. Samurais ought to be sharp."

You can hardly make efficient progress in a good idea

when your moods are confused. Provided that you feel un-committed and calm and mentally fresh, you can come to a conclusion in seven breaths. With your stomach set, you might be in a mood to smash your way through.

The Liked and the Disliked

Those who have gained a little learning soon become proud. They are pleased at being called men of consequence. They think themselves too good for their own generation. They think there are no higher people than they. Surely a divine punishment must inevitably fall upon their heads. However competent they may be, they are of no use if their colleagues do not like them and they cannot cooperate.

Those who like to be of help to others who even take delight in humbling themselves to work under the authority of their own colleagues—surely they are liked.

Conceal Your Wisdom

While doing service, it is without benefit to rise high while you are too young. However much gifted intelligence you may possess, people will refuse to recognize it if you are a greenhorn, because, at this time, your resource is not of a mature kind. You had better build up your brightness until the age of fifty or so, and then give it restrained play. The slower, the better.

Even if the ambitious and the loyal should go bad, they can restore their ruin quickly because they had not intended to profit through selfish motives.

Fall Seven Times and Get Up Eight

It is preposterous to feel upset when you are offered to be ronin. Those people who served in the reign of Lord Katsushige never failed to say, "You cannot be real samurais until you do ronin seven times. You must have seven falls and stand up eight times."

Hyogo Narutomi, I hear, actually became a ronin seven times. You must understand yourself as a Dharuma doll. A Lord ought to give leave to his samurais to try the ronin way.

Talk to Your Inferiors

A war poem about Yoshitsune (an old general) says, "Generals should often speak to their officers and men." You must talk to your subjects, not only in natural days (wartime), but also in ordinary days. Say: "You have done something worth while. How old a hand you are! Make more effort." They will work hard at the risk of their lives. After all, such words are most important.

How to Excel Above Others

The way to excel above others is to have others talk about you and judge you. The people of ordinary ability finish with their own narrow opinions about themselves and, therefore, there is no further development. To consult with others is a spring-board to a higher level.

A samurai was said to have shown his own official documents to others, and he would ask their opinions. Yet he was reputed to be the best samurai to compose this kind of official document. His work was perfect; yet the very fact that he asked others to look over his work meant that he already had surpassed them.

Bushido Alone Is the Way

It is evil that one object splits into two. You need only follow Bushido, the way of the samurai. There is no need to seek any other path.

Understand that the Chinese characters for Buddhism and Bushido are basically similar in that *do* means "the way." The same character is the sole way.

If you look at Bushido after learning Confucianism and Buddhism, the Bushido may seem quite unreasonable. But if you first learn the Bushido way and keep the Bushido perspective in mind, then you can fulfill the mastery of the other ways more effectively.

Honor and Wealth

For the most part, samurais who do not adhere to honor and wealth will abuse others and fall into cynicism. These samurais are useless compared to those who are deeply immersed in the pursuit of honor and wealth. The former are uselessly vain and proud to no purpose; they are quite irrelevant to the need of today.

On Homosexuality

Shikibu had a view: "Regarding homosexuality, young samurais might experience an error that will cause life-long shame. You are in danger if you lack proper understanding. Few people are in a position to talk and advise about this subject. Samurais have to bear the following in mind: a good 'wife' never meets a second 'husband.' The object of your love is one for life. Otherwise, you are the same as a prostitute. Too shameful for a samurai.

"It is truly said by Saikako Ihara (a writer) that 'A samurai without a companion is like a girl without a fiance.' People will ridicule such a samurai.

"After five years or so of intimacy, you will discover the ultimate conscience of your supposed companion; and then you can ask him to elevate the relationship.

"Inconstant samurais will not take root and will probably desert you in a short time. When you choose a guardian, you must prudently verify the root of his nature. Remember, you must be willing to throw away your lives for each other. If another should court you, shake him off with 'You stand in my way.' If he insists and asks, 'Who is the impediment?' answer him with 'I will never tell you as long as I live.' And if he persists, cut him down.

"As said before, you had better look into the motive of the younger companion. Five years' whole-hearted devotion to him will win him over. But at all events, never have two strings to your bow. At the same time, be assiduous in the practice of military arts while thus engaged. Thus your conduct will be consistent with Bushido."

How to Conduct Yourself

Even in jest, samurais should endeavor to never say anything that will reveal they are afraid. Nor should they take action hesitantly.

Your innermost heart can be revealed by your slip of the tongue—even if it is meant as a joke.

Spiritual Vigor

When Tsunetomo let Yasuburo draw calligraphy on fancy paper, he told him, "Assume that you are going to draw only one character on the whole paper. Then put it down as if your stroke would rip the paper. The result depends upon your spiritual vigor."

Samurais are best when they do not feel tired; this is the time when the work goes well.

The "Death" of Yamamoto

In view of the fact that some samurais serve until the age of sixty to seventy, my stay in the world, when I come to think of it, was rather too short. I renounced the world at the age of forty-two. Yet I am not sorry at all, but am rather content with my decision. For, even though I entered monkhood at the time and was resolved to throw away my life (in the world), now that I look back, I see how troublesome and cumbersome my life would have been if I had carried on (in the world) up until now.

I am unexpectedly fortunate to have been able to pass these fourteen years in comfort and ease. (While I was in life,) there existed some who patronized me as a somebody. But when I consider myself honestly, how skillfully I disguised myself. Their favors were as much obliging as they were irrelevant and unwelcome.

The Samurai Ideal of the Handsome Man

The mastery of correcting one's facial expression and appearance is to be carried out by constantly looking into a mirror.

When I changed my hairstyle at the age of thirteen, I remained indoors for about a year. The reason was that my relatives used to say, "That boy looks too bright. He may fail before too long. The Lord particularly hates those who appear bright."

I made up my mind to take this opportunity to modify my face; so I continuously consulted a mirror. After a year had passed, everyone said, "He looks a tired and sick man." I took this as the beginning of my service.

Most people do not accept young people who try to appear clever. Unless you appear stately and composed, you cannot be called handsome. Samurais should look respectful, sternly handsome, and calmly responsible.

Consulting Others

If you judge and manage every affair while depending only on your own small learning and wisdom, you will fall contrary to the Way of Heaven and become partial and evil. Looked at from an impartial standpoint (the side), this is foul, weak, narrow, and pointless.

If a good idea does not occur to you when you want it, you'd better talk the situation over with someone wiser than yourself. Since this person is not involved in your problem, he can make decisions frankly and without considering his own interest; and then the decisions are in accordance with the Way of Heaven. Looked at from the side, this is strong-rooted and seems foolproof. Such decisions are just like staunch and many-rooted trees. One man's wisdom is like a rootless tree.

Under Forty

Under forty years of age, stand off from wisdom and discretion. Preserve your vigor and energy beyond the usual type of person.

Depending on personality and rank, even those over forty must also have intensity of energy by which they can make things echo in others.

How to Acquire Talented People

Before Katsushige passed on his lordship to his son, Mitsushige, he gave him a note consisting of about twenty items. All of the items are the opinions of Naoshige, the Founder. In the note was a description of how Katsushige's father, Naoshige, advised his son during a father-to-son talk. At this time, Naoshige had a quite critical disease.

"In order to rule the nation, you had best have able men," Naoshige said. Whereupon his son asked, "Do you mean I have to pray to Buddha and the gods for the appearance of these men?"

The father replied, "After all, you pray to God for things beyond human power and endeavor. It is within our power to get talented people to appear."

"How then is it possible?" he again asked.

Naoshige answered, "Irrespective of any matter, things gather around him who loves them. If he loves flowers, every variety of flower will begin to gather together about him, even though he has not had a single seed until that time. And, in due course, there will grow a flower of the rarest kind. Likewise, if you love people, the result will be the same. Make a point of loving and respecting."

Expressing the Spirit

For samurais, one word on the spot is most important. Through this one word, bravery manifests itself. In other words, in the days of peace, it is no other than your words that express your courage. Even in turbulent times, it was thought that you could tell a brave soldier from a coward by his one word. This one word is the flower of your spirit. It is beyond oratory explanation.

Giving and Receiving Advice

There are many in the world who are eager to give advice. There are few who feel glad for being given advice. And there are still fewer who follow the given advice.

No one will try to admonish you when you grow older than thirty. Consequently, you will grow more willful due to lack of warning. The result is that you repeat wrongdoings and you add to your folly throughout the rest of your life. Then you go to no good.

So take every opportunity to get familiar with the "way-knowing" people and learn lessons from them.

Accomplishment in the Arts and Crafts

Those who are reputed to be good at arts and crafts are good in a foolish fashion. They have become good at one particular subject because they foolishly became fond of and attached to one art without any regard to other matters. Quite useless.

BOOK TWO

Persuasion Tactics

When you meet someone for the first time, be quick to judge his character. Deal with him according to your observations. For example, if you meet an aggressive and argumentative person, be flexible; without being too unbending, you have to talk him down while making use of higher reason. And make sure there can be no grudge on his part. This is how your heart and words should work.

"Yes" Men

Good-natured men (i.e., obedient "yes" men) fall behind their colleagues. One should be full of energy and vitality.

How to Treat Your Superiors

In coping with a spirited, bright, and cheerful Lord, you have to make sure that he will perform his duty without blunder. You have to cheer him up by words of praise. This is done in order to bring him up to a strong disposition of spirit.

But with an unyielding and bright Lord, you must manage to let him acknowledge your superiority. Remind him of this consideration: "What will he think if he hears of my deed or my conduct or my decision?" This is the greatest loyalty and service you can render him. If there are no subjects to give him this kind of service, the Lord may hold all his subjects as inferior; then he will look down upon all of them as hand-rubbing people. Then he will rise high on his own self-pride.

However high or low they are and whatever good they do for the government, the pride of the Lord will undermine their deeds. Few are alive to this fact; the exceptions are Kyuma Sagara and Kichiemon Harada, who were alive to this kind of matter. Harada remained a consultant to the Lord, even in illness, and after his retirement. This was very useful to the Lord. Only if you think it is difficult to train yourself to give this kind of service does it really become difficult.

It is also my own experience that, if you break your bones to make effort, you will be able to succeed. Because this position (of a Lord's counsellor) is the only elite one, those who do not want this office are cowards. The models are Nobukata Itagaki and Takatomo Akimoto.

And if you should be hated by your Lord for giving him excessive advice, then you cannot fulfill your loyalty. This is the most important point that everyone misses. You proceed to let your Lord learn little by little.

On Serious Thoughts

After all, there is nothing else than concentrated thought for each moment. One serious thought piled upon another leads to a whole life. If you become aware only of this, there is nothing more to seek after. You have to keep to this single, concentrated thought alone. But everyone, losing hold of this point, seeks another place—only to fail to discover this truth. Now, in order not to let this idea of one serious thought leak out of your heart, you have to have diligence and merits and experience. But if once you have succeeded in arriving at this truth, it will always be in your heart, even though you may neglect to put it into everyday practice. If you truly understand this point, there will be no emergency. Within this serious thought, loyalty is inherent.

A Little Learning

A man of a little learning tends to criticize the present times. It is the beginning of his misfortune. Those who hold their tongues are favored in good times and remain unpunished in bad times.

How to Get Useful Ideas

When you hear others talk, listen to them earnestly as if their talk were rich in substance, however empty it sounds to you, so that they will not hesitate to tell you whatever is in their minds. Let them talk freely and without interruption.

Father's Favorite Sayings

The following are some of my father, Jin'emon Yamamoto's, favorite sayings:

"Dog's skin for inside the home, tiger's skin for outside."

"As your pen will not break from writing 'Sincerely yours,' no matter how often, so your neck will not break from making a bow." (You lose nothing by being polite.)

"Spur even rushing horses."

"Telling seven lies before going a block makes a man of you."

A Samurai Esprit de Corps

During the Korean campaign, the Nabeshima troops were camping in Korai, Korea. The then Lord Naoshige, looking down from a hill, saw a group of his soldiers enjoying a rest with their hoods (to defend against arrows) off. He became angry and said, "This is a battlefield! It is too careless of them. Send to find out who was the first to take off the hood. He shall be punished."

The messenger went and asked for the explanation. The soldiers were embarrassed and did not know what to say. Now Heigozaemon Koyama, one of the soldiers, came up with a good idea and said to the messenger, "The twenty of us all took off our hoods at exactly the same moment." This answer disarmed Naoshige and so no one was punished.

The Present and the Past

The wind of the times is unchangeable. This wind shows that the world has entered into a stage of degeneration and that society is gradually being corrupted. But it is impossible for a spring or a summer to last for the whole year. This is also true of one day. Accordingly, you cannot restore the good old days and customs and fashions of a hundred years ago.

It is, therefore, essential to do your best according to the requirements of the present generation. In refusing to accept this with resignation, nostalgic people are grossly mistaken. Indeed, they are very unreasonable in a childish way. On the other hand, those who can only think of the present trend and hate the signs of older times cannot hope to acquire retrospective knowledge.

Make the Best of Each Occasion

It is said that Kenshin Uesugi (reputed to be one of the greatest generals in the Age of Civil Wars) once remarked: "I don't know the knack of victory at all times. I have only learned how not to miss the right moment."

Significant remark, indeed!

O, What a Vain World

As I was walking along, a thought came to me: human beings are just like naturally operated marionettes! Without any strings they walk, skip, jump, even speak. How well wrought they are! At the Bon Festival next year, perhaps many of them will be guests (spirits, already dead). O, what a useless, futile world! They simply forget this perspective completely.

Handling Negative Feelings

If you say, "O, what a pity, etc." to those who are agitated and overcome due to an unforeseen disaster, they will be choked with more grief and will become even more addled. When this happens, just say casually, "It is ultimately good that this has happened." In this way you are in a position to divert them from their grief and annoyance. In due course, they will begin to take to your remarks and recover their reason.

In this rapidly changing world, it is not necessary to hang onto either sorrow or delight.

Samurai's Toilette

You'd better carry rouge and powder in your bosom, as the occasion demands. For instance, in the event of recovering from intoxication or of awakening from sleep, you may look pale. In such case, you can apply rouge and powder to your cheeks for an important occasion.

At the Conference

As for conferences: Gather everyone concerned together. Listen to their opinions; then make a quick and decisive decision. Otherwise, someone will surely appear offended

As for important matters: Let outsiders and laymen comment in confidence. Since they will be disinterested, they will be able to see things objectively and with more reason.

If you confer only with people in your own circle (relatives and friends), their opinions will naturally favor you, rendering them useless.

Deny the Gods if They Stand in Your Way

Although I am told that the gods dislike the defiled—still—out of my own trivial strategy, I have never failed to pray every day, even to these gods.

I pray to the gods simply for my good luck when I am working under a rain of blood and jumping over the dead bodies. I pray to the gods without regard for the gods' dislike of bloodstain. I think that it cannot be helped if they turn away from me because I am bloodstained.

Human Life Is Trivial

Life of humankind is indeed very short and trifling. You ought to spend your time doing whatever you like to do. It is very foolish to lead your life troubling yourself with unfavorable matters in this world of dream.

If this is misinterpreted, it will harm youth. So I have not spoken of this to the young samurais. This is my secret, from my own inner shrine (i.e., this is playing my trump card). I personally like to sleep. I am thinking of sleeping away the rest of my life, permitting my legs to work only as much as my present circumstances require.

You Cannot Tell Your Own Ability

Kaion Osho (monk Kaion) once said, "Those people who see very little think they are awakened to their own merits and demerits. Therefore, self-praise springs up within them. Indeed, it is still impossible for you to know your length and width; you cannot judge yourself."

Dignity

The way you look is literally the expression of your own dignity. Your dignity can find expression in many ways: in your efforts; in your graceful, mild manners; in the calm and silence of your bearing; in your grave conduct; and in your piercing stare effected with clenched teeth. These are all expressions of your inner dignity. After all, the fundamental lies in your being seriously aware with total concentration of mind.

Don't Despise the "Upstarts"

Kazuma Nakano once told me, "There are some who deem it squalid to use an old bowl at tea ceremony. They think new bowls are clean and better."

On the other hand, there are those who consider the use of old bowls to be proper. They are both wrong: what are now known as old bowls have found their way through the hands of the humble into the hands of the great solely by virtue of their inherent value.

This is also the case with servants. It is simply because of their own ability that they are able to rise from low estate to high. It is a gross mistake for you to refuse to share a post of equal rank with them or not to agree to receive those who have no family background. You must not refuse our superiors on the ground that they were formerly the light-legged. You must respect those who have climbed from the lowly more than you do the wellborn people who remain in high posts.

Keeping a Respectful Distance

Unless a samurai allows his Lords, Chief Retainers, and elders to keep him at a respectful distance, he cannot carry out great assignments. He cannot work effectively when he is reduced to being their shadow. Always bear this in mind.

Weigh Your Words

It's a great fault to speak of others' affairs. It is also not advisable to praise others. After all, it is most important to know your own self and apply yourself to your own self-mastery. You had better weigh your words.

Two Kinds of People

Virtuous people are relaxed in their minds. They do not seem to be busy about anything. The little men are very noisy; they make a fuss, argue, and rattle around.

Defeating Yourself by Victory

On the occasion of lawsuits, discussion, and debates, there are some cases in which you can lose all the more splendidly if you withdraw your opinions earlier than expected. It is like Japanese wrestling: if you are too eager for victory and win foully, then your victory is worse than a true victory; rather your foul victory will turn into a foul defeat.

On Visiting Others

When you decide to call on others for a talk, you had better notify them of your impending visit, as it may be that they are otherwise occupied. Or your visit could prove embarrassing if they have something else on their mind. After all, you need not go where you have not been invited. Because one can have few bosom friends, even if your apparent friends should invite you, you may feel ill at ease in their company. If you see them only at parties at long intervals, you will not be able to open your heart in their company. Generally speaking, you are liable to blunder at the entertainment seat.

On the other hand, it would not be good for you to avoid meeting your visitors when they drop by and you are busily involved.

Analogy of the Sword

A samurai once said, "There are only two kinds of willpower: one is within and the other is without. If you don't show it (the willpower) at the right moment, then it is useless."

Let me draw an analogy, that of the sword blade: when you occasionally draw the sword out to wipe it, you had better whet the blade, hold it at eyebrow height, and then put it back again in its sheath. On the other hand, if you always keep your sword out of its sheath and swing it about, then no one will come near you and you will have no friends. But if you keep it always in its sheath, then your sword will become dull with rust; then people will underestimate you.

Talent and the Times

We sometimes fail to accomplish great works by being too impetuous. By thinking there are "miles yet to go," you can reach your goal or object all the sooner. In other words, your "season of completion" arrives by itself. Let's think fifteen years ahead: the world will have totally changed by that time.

Although there are books of forecasts in our country, they have nothing particularly new in them.

And many who are useful now will have died in fifteen years. More than half of the youth presently living will be dead. It is as if, in proportion to the gradual degeneration of the age, silver becomes all important when gold runs out. And when silver runs out, copper becomes the treasure. Likewise, in due course, human ability will slow down with the degeneration of society. So, if you only encourage yourself to pursue those who are ahead of you, you will find yourself still suitable for service in fifteen years. After all, fifteen years is a comparatively short period of time. And if only you take good care of your health, then you can reach your aim and become useful. This would be very difficult in times when there are many talented people. Yet it will be easy to distinguish yourself among the new generation in the corrupt age that is developing.

Listening to Veterans

When you hear a veteran talk, listen to him carefully, even though he may tell you what you already know. In due course, as you listen to the same story ten times and twenty times, the moment will come when you suddenly understand the point you have been missing. You can take this point to heart. At that time, your understanding will deepen. So don't explain away these stories as just the tedious talk of old folk; rather, think of old people as the experienced ones.

Drop Out Completely

Only the "thrown-away" who have descended to the depths will prove useful in the time of need. But those people who can only do one particular task well will be useless.

Samurais:
Men of Action

As I have already recorded in my book *Stupid Opinions,* the ultimate objective is to reach the position of Chief Retainer and express opinions to the Lord. But few people have understood this. If only you could truly understand this fact, the rest can be overlooked. How few men of character there are! By chance, there may be flatterers who fawn on superiors in quest of advancement based on their self-interest. But this type is small and selfish and is not ambitious enough to hope to achieve the position of Chief Retainer. Even those who have at least some self-possession and who are able to remain detached from profit and desire—even they do not step into the extreme of service. They enjoy reading *Tsurezuregusa* by Kenko and *Senshusho* by Saigyo. But these two ex-samurais are waist-disjointed cowards. Cowards because they could not fulfill the requisites of samurais and so they pretended to live the lives of hermits. Nowadays, bonzes (monks) and elderly people may be justified in reading such works. But samurais must be serviceable to the Lord; they must jump into the midst of the world of profit and honor and, if necessary, run through the hell (of egocentric calculation and self-interest).

The Family Grant

Tsunetomo said to his adopted son, Gonnojo, "The youth of today have become effeminate. The day has come when people mistakenly praise the good-natured (weak, smiling characters) and the affable as smooth and gentle fellows. So they tend not to reach far enough nor do they cleave their way to their goal.

"Their spirits wither because they strongly adhere to their grants and are afraid to lose them. You may think that you must never destroy the fief of the family that you were adopted into. You may think that your forefathers have taken great pains to achieve this grant. But this is only a tendency of the society. My views are quite different. While I was actively giving myself to service, I thought nothing of the grant. From the beginning, the grant belongs to the Lord. We need not spare it nor grudge it, nor think it important. It will be extremely satisfying if we have an opportunity to do ronin and harakiri connected with our service during our lifetime. It is these two—ronin and harakiri—and nothing more that lead to the end of samurais."

Still, it will be deplorable and regrettable to allow one's house to crumble for trivial reasons. Therefore, you must never defile yourself by lagging behind your fellow samurai; by being an inadequate samurai; by acting according to self-desire; by doing harm to your colleagues. If you happen to bring your house to ruin for other reasons, this is quite acceptable. If you are thus determined, your hand reaches itself far, your power becomes truly full, and you can do your work with great energy.

On Servants

Mimasaku Taku, in his old age, treated his servants very severely and made excessive demands on them. Someone eventually admonished him for this habit. But he answered, "It is for the sake of my son. He must be able to sleep with a calm conscience after my death."

Generally speaking, when the former master has driven his servants hard and treated them mercilessly before he retired, the servants become more quickly attached to the present head of the house.

A Koan on the Art of Homosexuality

Ryotetsu Hoshino was the pioneer of the homosexual relationship in our country. In spite of great numbers of students, he imparted the knowledge to them both individually and privately.

Edayoshi (one of his students) eventually discovered the

secret of this particular art. When he was ordered to accompany the Lord to Yedo, (now Tokyo), he had to take leave of Ryotetsu, his master.

Ryotetsu questioned him: "What is your understanding of the love between young samurais?"

Edayoshi answered, "It is something to like and yet not to like."

Ryotetsu was glad to hear this reply and added, "How many pains have I taken to bring you up to this level of understanding!"

Some years later, a samurai asked the "why" of the above statement that Edayoshi made. Edayoshi answered, "The secret of this art is to throw away your life for your partner; otherwise your relation will be shameful. But if you do throw away your life for your partner, then there is no life anymore to devote to your Lord himself. That's why I answered in such a manner."

The Connection Game

It is a defect on the part of subjects to make a pilgrimage to their superiors. If you have any kind of good backing, you are not free to speak. No matter how hard you may assert yourself and be elevated in position, others will point a finger of scorn at you. They will say, "He is happy to be taken care of—thanks to influence." Then your whole-hearted service comes to nothing. You can work freely and effectively without "pull" of any sort.

On the Spur of Madness

Being that you are samurais, be proud of your valor and prowess and prepare yourself to die with frenzy.

Keep in mind to purify your everyday diction, thinking, deportment, and the like. And try hard to do it.

The way to serve is to consult with people you can confide in. Speak with unconcerned people about important affairs. And also realize that you are to devote your lifelong services to the interest of others. It is better for you not to know general information.

Handling Difficulties

There is a saying: "If the water rises, the ship rises, too." In other words, in dealing with a problem that you are especially good at handling, the more difficult the problem is, the higher your talents and willingness will rise in order to cope with the difficulties. You must not hesitate; if you do so, this will make all the difference in the result.

On Dreams

Dreams are the honest expression of your inner person. I have often dreamt of fighting to death, and of harakiri. As I gradually got used to the dreams and felt at ease with them, my feelings (in the dreams) changed and they now flow much easier.

The Samurai Ideal of Love

The extreme attitude of love is a secret feeling of love. It is like this:

I will love to death, with my inner thoughts never revealed;

Let others know it by (my) death smoke.

It is no longer a deep love if you allow it to be revealed during your lifetime. The extent of love is limitlessly long when you carry through with your love till death. Even if the other person asks you, "Isn't it this?" ("Isn't it that you love me?") you answer her by, "Such a thing has never entered my head."

Dying in love is the highest form of love. This is really a roundabout way (of love). When I last spoke with some samurais, they shared this opinion (of mine), and they decided to call themselves the "smoke group." This attitude can also be applied to many other matters, for example, between the Lord and subject samurais. This way of mind is sufficient for almost any purpose.

BOOK THREE

Collapsing House

Naoshige, the founder of the Nabeshima clan, spoke to his grandson, Motoshige, "Whether it is high or low, the house and the clan will collapse when its time comes. At that moment, if you resist the course, a foul collapse will result. If you are aware that the time has come, you had better let your house crumble without hesitation. On the other hand, if you have this foresight, you might be able to hold your house back in your arms."

Story of the Thwarted Ghosts

After an investigation, Naoshige put to death the samurai and the woman who committed secret intercourse in the third circle of the castle.

Later, their ghosts walked by night within the castle. The

maidservants were so scared that they did not dare to leave their rooms at night.

Some time passed before the Lady Naoshige heard of the haunting. Then she asked someone to pray for exorcism and to celebrate a mass for the repose of their dead souls. Yet all of these efforts proved to no purpose. So the matter was finally reported to Lord Naoshige himself.

Lord Naoshige said, "I am extremely glad of this. They deserved more than just decapitation. I hold their sin so execrable that I am glad that they cannot go where they should have gone but still have to haunt in ghost forms. I am very pleased that they still suffer for their misconduct and remain restless. It is, indeed, quite understandable that they have haunted this long."

From that night on, the ghosts stopped appearing.

BOOK FOUR

Four Kinds of Samurai

Lord Katsushige used to remark, "There are four kinds of subjects: the alert-alert, the dull-alert, the alert-dull, and the dull-dull.

"Alert-alert are those who are very quick on the uptake when they are told to do something. They arrange affairs and carry out duties in a fine manner. They are so good that they are few in number. Kichizaemon Fukuchi is nearly on this level.

"Dull-alert are those people who fail to clearly understand at first what their duty is. But, in finally putting their duty into practice, they perform splendidly and with no delay. Kazuma Nakano is this kind.

"Alert-dull are those people who, when told to do something, accept very graciously and willingly, but they take a long time to fulfill the task. There are many such samurai.

"The rest are dull-dull. They are in the majority."

Saving Face

When Lord Katsushige was hunting at Shiraishi, he shot a big boar. Everyone ran up to it and looked at it closely. They said, "Our Lord has shot unusually big game." All of a sudden, the boar rose to its feet and began to run. In total confusion, the onlookers ran off in all directions.

Meanwhile, Matabei Nabeshima whipped out a sword and slashed at the boar with a single movement. The animal was slain.

During this time, Lord Katsushige raised his sleeve up to cover his eyes. "Dust rises!" he exclaimed. This was done in this manner in order not to see his samurais upset.

BOOK FIVE

Humility of the Lord

On his initial leave, Lord Tsunashige went for the first time down to his province. He was accompanied by his father, Lord Mitsushige. Hearing that the Lord's son had returned for the first time, the people of the villages knelt down on either side of the street and bowed deeply while the palanquins passed them by.

Later, Tsunashige told his father about this.

"You must know better," his father answered in a severe tone. "You must not think you are worth being kowtowed to!"

BOOK SIX

Compassion and Courage

Monk Tannen usually pointed out, "It is impossible for a monk to achieve Buddha's way unless, within himself, he is overflowing with courage; and, at the same time, he must keep the outward display of being compassionate. . . ."

A samurai cannot fulfill his duty unless he has enough compassion within to break his stomach; at the same time, he must appear courageous without. Consequently, a monk learns courage from a samurai and a samurai imbibes compassion from the monk.

For several years, I have pursued my studies of Buddhism while walking about in different countries. Although I visited many a so-called erudite monk, I have not been able to learn anything from them that proved useful to my studies. But, on the other hand, whenever I heard that there lived a hero samurai, I went out of my way—through a lot of travel difficulties—just to hear him talk about Bushido.

His talk always turned out to be rewarding and useful to my own research in Buddhism.

First of all, samurais can run into the enemy's camps with the help of arms and swords that they carry. But how is it possible for monks with only beads in hand to run through spears and swords? Can they do this only with their tenderness and feeling of compassion? They cannot dash into the enemy's camp without great courage. In view of this, it is not difficult to understand why a monk shakes from nervousness when he burns incense at a Buddhist service in the presence of great people. He shakes simply because he lacks boldness and courage. It requires a lot of spirit to kick the rising dead down again to hell, just as it does to raise some out of hell (elevate sentient beings).

It is a great pity that most monks today take (interest in) irrelevant things. They want to appear meek and to behave sanctimoniously. They, therefore, seldom achieve the spirit of Buddhism. More than this, it is deplorable that monks advise samurais to learn Buddhism. Thereby they make waist-disjointed cowards out of the samurais. It is outrageous for young samurais to listen to Buddhism; because then your object (Bushido) gets divided. Samurais are useless unless they are out and out oriented to Bushido. Old, retired samurais may very well listen to Buddhism for their playtime or leisure, but not so active ones.

Samurais ought to carry poles on their shoulders and put as much loyalty and filial piety in each basket as they put courage and compassion in the other basket. The beam should dig into their shoulders for twenty-four hours each day.

Either at morning or evening prayer, or when you stay at home or go out or sit or lie, recite, "My Lord, My Lord." Then divine providence is as much with you as when you recite the name of Buddha or the sutras. If you believe in patron deities, then your fortune grows strong. Also, compassion is like a mother rearing the child of fortune. It is evident through old and new examples that samurais with only courage, but without compassion, become extinct.

BOOK SEVEN

To Kill

Kichizaemon Yamamoto (the author's brother) learned under the guidance of his father how to hack dogs. He did this at the age of five. And at the age of fifteen, he learned how to hack criminals.

It was a requisite for samurais of old to cut off heads before they reached fourteen or fifteen years of age.

Lord Katsushige, when very young, learned to cut under the direction of his father, Lord Naoshige. In due course, he could slaughter ten people on end. It is unwise not to have the children of the common (samurais) kill at all. In olden days, even the upper (Lord) engaged in this activity. Most of the samurais today say, "It is useless," or "It is not meritorious to cut bound men," or "It is foul and dirty." These are all excuses. In short, it would appear that their real intention is to polish their nails and to keep respectability, but the truth is that they fall short of the practice of the military profession.

If we inquire into their disposition, we see that they make excuses not to kill by hiding behind a cloak of words. The reason they do this is that they expect they will feel uneasy at the deed.

Because it is a thing for samurais to do, Naoshige coached his son. I, myself, some years ago, cut at the execution grounds at Kase. And I felt comfortable and enlivened. Thinking of it as uncomfortable is just a symptom of inner cowardice.

The Loyal Samurai Cook

When Lord Katsushige entertained his guest with some dishes of crane, Kichizaemon Fukuchi acted in the following manner:

A guest said, "Your honorable host, I hear that you can taste the difference between white cranes and black cranes, etc. Is this true?"

The Lord replied, "It is true."

The guest went on, "Then, how have you tasted the present dish?"

Katsushige answered, "That was a white-naped crane."

The guest replied, "I don't understand how you can tell the difference. Please send for the cook. I want to ask him."

"Let Kichizaemon Fukuchi come," the Lord said.

Kichizaemon, who had overheard the discussion, quickly went into the kitchen and drank, in succession, several big bowls of sake (rice wine). He was repeatedly requested to come (before the Lord). After some time, he went into the presence (of the Lord and guest). Then the guest repeated his question. Kichizaemon's tongue tripped and he lisped in a foolish manner: "White-black crane, nay, pure-white crane or black crane."

The Lord scolded him, "You are drunk. Get out of my sight." (Thus the Lord's face was saved.)

To Win Is to Overcome Yourself

Hyogo Narutomi once said, "To win is to overcome your own side. To win, your own side must overcome itself. To win one's self is to overcome the body with the mind. Unless you train your spirit and your body every day to such an extent that there is none comparable to you among the tens of thousands of samurais on your side, it will be impossible for you to defeat your enemies."

The Essence of Service

Oribe Ikuno (Chief Retainer to Lord Mitsushige) taught me a lesson: I, Tsunetomo, in my youth would take a nightcap at the castle before going to bed. One night, as I was drinking, Oribe said to me, "Because Shogen Nakano (a relative of Tsunetomo) asked me to instruct you in the knowledge of service, and because we are intimate, I shall tell you.

"I don't know anything about it, but it is not difficult to

understand that samurais can work willingly when they are employed in an efficient place of business. But they sometimes tend to sulk when they are reduced to a more menial office. This is no good. Quite ungrateful.

"The essence of service is that good-positioned samurais should more willingly draw the water from the well and cook the rice. They should perform these humble tasks in high spirits; and they should not begrudge those who ask them. This is what I've found out. Please keep this in mind as you seem too aggressive and active for someone of your tender age."

A Story Concerning Lord Tsunashige

When Gorozaemon Yamamoto (nephew to the author) was assigned to the Yedo office, he challenged the bonze (monk) Kaion (who was a Zen prelate at Mt. Kurotaki). Here is the story:

When Lord Tsunashige was still dependent (upon his father, i.e., not yet a Lord), he became a disciple to Kaion and learned the teachings of Buddha.

It was rumored on the premises (i.e., the branch office of the Nabeshima clan in Yedo) that the Lord was to be given a certificate indicating that he had attained to a certain point of wisdom. This is known as "Inka" in Zen Buddhism.

At this time, Gorozaemon had been appointed attendant

to the Lord and functioned also as a superintendent officer. Hearing of the rumor, he visited Kaion at his Yedo residence. Disapproving of the certificate, he intended to prevent Kaion from giving it. He was ready to cut the monk down if Kaion would not comply with his wishes.

When he asked for an interview, Kaion came out in a very dignified and stately manner, for he thought Yamamoto came to pay his homage.

Gorozaemon said, "I have a secret matter to be discussed privately. Please order the room to be cleared of all attendant monks." When this had been done, he advanced on Kaion and continued, "I have heard that our Lord is going to be awarded a certificate for his clear understanding of the doctrines of Buddhism. As you also come from Hizen, I take it that you are familiar with most of the customs and traditions of both the Ryuzoz and Nabeshima clans. As distinct from other clans, our clan has lasted for generations and it has been customary with us for both high and low to cooperate to govern the country with all classes of people in perfect union.

"It is unprecedented that any Lord of our clan should receive such a certificate. If you bestow it now, Lord Tsunashige will slight the counsel of clansmen as coming from clods; he will feel proud that he has achieved satori, because men of rank are apt to be conceited.

"Assure me positively that you will never give this certificate to the Lord. Unless you consent, I will have to take a resolute step."

The monk, who had been listening to him, was fast losing his color. But he answered the request, "How admirable your heart! I shall keep your opinion about your household in mind. You are indeed a loyal subject."

Gorozaemon retorted, "That's your old trick; I know it well. I have not come for praise. My point is whether you suspend the certificate or not. I want a definite reply: 'yes' or 'no.'"

The monk replied, "It is quite reasonable for you to say this. I shall never give (the Lord) the certificate."

Since Kaion made the pledge, Gorozaemon returned home; but first, before leaving the monk's residence, he reminded the monk again about the matter of the certificate.

I (Tsunetomo) personally heard this from Gorozaemon.

BOOK EIGHT

About Kichinosuke Shida

(Note: This samurai, Kichinosuke, avoided giving service to a second Lord so that he could remain loyal to the memory of his first Lord, who had died. The author speaks of him in an admiring tone.)

About Kichinosuke Shida: Kichinosuke had waited on Masaie Ryuzozi as a page boy. When the reign of Katsushige began, he adopted a son and transferred to him the leadership of his house; then he left his business and lived in easy retirement.

Mimasaku Taku was on intimate terms with him and called on him frequently. They were very close. Kichinosuke being a man of highest calibre, Mimasaku privately consulted with him on all matters. He intended to advise the Lord to give him a big stipend and assign him to an important post. Kichinosuke divined his intentions, pretended to be a fool, and made himself seem like a greedy character.

Kichinosuke began to deal in eye lotion; he put many things into hock; he performed a dance. He would walk past a vicious dog with the end of his kimono tucked up. Then he would say, "A wound in the leg might heal itself, but a hurt in a kimono cannot heal!"

Sensing that he was merely playing the part of a fool, Mimasaku intensified his wish to make him serve. In turn, Kichinosuke made himself seem a great coward: he would run under a torii. Whenever he walked along the bank of a moat, he would walk under the roof of the wall. To top it all off, he walked on the other side of the bank saying, "I do this because, when I meet a murderer, I'll be able to throw myself into the water and save my precious life." Or he would say, "I prefer crucifixion to decapitation because death by crucifixion is much slower than decapitation. And I'd like to live a little longer—even if just a little longer. If there is not much difference between life and death, I would prefer to live."

All this (he said and did) in order to avoid service. And he successfully avoided service throughout his life.

Once on his way to Chikugo to sell eye lotion, he met a gang of bandits in the mountains. He cut them down and drove the other two away by wounding them. Although he kept this event secret, the truth gradually came out. And everyone praised him: "Well done! He must be an old fox."

To this rumor he explained, "Not an old fox but a mere coward. Because I really wanted to save my own life—that's why I cut the others down just a moment before they would have slain me."

Other events of a similar nature frequently occurred: he once collected gold and silver and hid it in a ditch. He later placed it in a hole in the pillar and hung it from a beam.

In the evening of his life, he erected a gate to the temple of Ryutai-Ji. And he built himself a hermitage near a mausoleum of the Lord Masaic. There he perished.

At the beginning of Lord Mitsushige's rule, Mimasaku talked with Kichinosuke. Mimasaku said, "Administration is important when there is a change of leadership. I have taken notes on what Lord Katsushige said when alive. Listen to them and follow them carefully. I shall be reading them to the rest later on."

Mimasaku had read two or three clauses when Kichinosuke said, "I'm feeling bored so I'm leaving."

Becoming insulted, Mimasaku asked him why he felt bored.

"I expected you to be an average Chief Retainer," he replied, "but I've found you useless. It is the Chief Retainer's duty to make sure every subject is attached to a Lord. But if you should show them the present document, they will yearn for the deceased Lord even more eagerly, and they will applaud his accomplishments. It is only a short time since the former Lord passed away. The tears of the devoted samurais have not yet dried. At this time, if such a document should be presented before them, they will miss him all the more. Then they will hardly take to the present Lord. They are anxious about the present Lord, who was born in Yedo, and who is a sort of stranger among his retainers. If you think of yourself as a loyal and wise official, make this document known to them as if it were written by the present Lord. Never let on your designs. And they will then form a better opinion of him as being a Lord superior to the deceased Katsushige. And they will grow attached to the new Lord right from the beginning."

At this, Mimasaku said, "You are quite right. This is why I have shown this to you alone." Then he tore the document into pieces right on the spot.

About the Promotion of Ichiemon Kuno

About the promotion for Ichiemon Kuno: since Ichiemon was exceptionally useful, Lord Katsushige had been thinking of advancing him. But it so happened that Ichiemon and Shigesato (Katsushige's brother-in-law) were on bad terms with each other. So, in deference to his brother-in-law, Shigesato, Lord Katsushige put off his advancement. In the meantime, it was decided that Katsushige would visit Ichiemon's house.

On hearing the problem, Shigesato said to Katsushige, "Ichiemon is a very useful samurai; on this occasion it is natural that he should be promoted."

Katsushige was very glad to hear this, sent for Ichiemon at once, and promptly promoted him, saying, "I am relieved that Shigesato changed his mind about you. Now go and express your gratitude to him."

Ichiemon light-heartedly called on Shigesato. He went immediately and expressed his deep gratitude for the latter's help. He also thanked him for the 300 mats that Shigesato had presented to him in preparation for the coming of Lord Katsushige.

In answer, Shigesato said, "Because you have been earnestly employed in your service, I advised the Lord about your advancement. Also, because the Lord was going to visit you, I gave you the mats. But this does not mean that I have become reconciled with you. Get out of here at once. Never come to my house again in your life. Give the mats back."

And he actually took back the mats. Later on, when Shigesato was about to die, he called Ichiemon to him and said, "To tell the truth, it seemed at that time that you were prone to self-conceit and haughtiness. But you were really a sharp-edged fellow. Therefore, I purposely pretended during my life to be hostile toward you only in order to subdue your excessiveness. After my death there will be no one to control you. Train yourself to be humble and modest and be of service to the Lord—as you have always done till now."

Ichiemon returned home, eyes wet with tears of gratitude.

How to Restore the Clan After It Collapses

Doko Anju narrated: "When the hereditary vassals happen to have for themselves a Lord or Chief Retainer who is full of injustice and makes frequent errors, the samurais must be posted on (informed of) the gate of revival (restoration of the clan). If the administration is inefficient and our country should pass into the hands of another clan, we must reclaim it to the Nabeshima clan. I call this method 'the gate of revival.'

"First of all, you must previously (i.e., before the clan is even in any danger of being abolished) make the youngest son of the Lord enter into the priesthood. In the same manner, each samurai ought also to let all his sons, except the eldest, become either monks or farmers. Then when it happens that a new Lord (with his retainers) is transferred to our country, every farmer and every priest previously disguised can assemble and combine efforts to spread false rumors of injustice by the new Lord. This can give birth to public censure in various ways. And it can force the new Lord to be exiled from the country. After the same policy is repeated a few times, priests and farmers (in disguise) can sue the Shogunate Government and appeal in the following way:

"Since Hizen (name for the land of the Nabeshima clan) is a country of hereditary succession, the people do not at all take to the new Lord. Rather, they miss the former Lord.

"Even if the Shogunate Government should appoint new Lords one after another, these Lords will not be able to last long.

"As it happens, there is an offspring of the former Lord here. This son is now a priest. Therefore, if he is ordered to return to secular life and to take pity on (i.e., govern) the country of Hizen—then the whole nation is sure to be governed well!"

Then the clan can survive.

Doko, for his part, saw to it that the second son was a priest and the third son a farmer.

Cut Down the Gods if They Stand in Your Way

Shigekata Nabeshima scolded his son. Here is what happened: The son sent a message to his father. The message said, "I would like to pay a visit to Atago Shrine in Kyoto."

Hearing this, Shigekata asked the messenger, "For what purpose?"

The messenger replied, "Atago Gongen, being the god of bow and arrow (war), he has set his mind upon prayer to Gongen for success in warfare."

Shigekata angrily replied, "Quite unnecessary! Why should the Nabeshima vanguard rely upon Atago Gongen? Be resolved to slice his body into two pieces and walk between them if he (Gongen) confronts us on the side of the enemy."

Two Kinds of Samurais

My father used to say only this to his servants (samurais): "Gamble and tell lies; unless you can tell seven lies as you walk a cho (a block, or 119 yards), you cannot show your manliness."

He said this because he thought good-mannered samu-rais usually failed to achieve great work. He also said this be-cause formerly (i.e., in time of war) valor and vigor alone were treasured. He connived with his misbehaving samurais and left them unpunished saying, "You have done well."

Kyuma Sagara also overlooked retainers who committed theft and adultery. Gradually he made samurais out of them. He said, "Only this kind of samurai can develop to be really useful."

BOOK NINE

A Samurai
and His Adulterous Wife

A samurai once put his wife to the sword. When he returned home, he found his wife and retainer engaging in illicit intercourse in the bedroom. As soon as he entered the room, the servant (samurai) ran away into the kitchen.

He immediately killed his wife with his sword. Then he called one of the maids and explained the circumstances. He said to her, "Work together with me so that everyone will think the death was caused by disease. Otherwise it will bring shame on my children. If you hesitate, you shall die for complicity."

She answered, "As long as you spare my life, I will arrange things so that no truth may be made known."

Then she put some bedclothes over the body.

Later, two or three requests were made for a doctor. The

doctor was sent for under the pretense of there being a dangerous illness. Then, eventually, a messenger was sent saying that, since it was all over (i.e., the wife had died), there was no need for the doctor to have come. The samurai called the wife's uncle and persuaded him of the same fact. So he managed to pretend to the end that the death had been a natural one. Nothing else was ever revealed.

Later on, he gave leave to the retainer. This happened at Yedo, I hear.

BOOK TEN

How Not to Get Nervous

Before you attend an important occasion, apply spit to your earlobe and then breathe in deeply through your nostrils. Then go out. Kick every object you come across. This is the secret.

Again, when you feel dizzy, apply spit to your earlobe and you will come to your senses instantly.

How to Win in a Debate

When you argue in a lawsuit, you had better say, "I will answer later after more consideration." Even if you have made your subject clear from the beginning to end, you may do well to leave the room after making some excuse. Do this by saying, "I will think about it some more."

And it would be better to tell this and that friend the details of the lawsuit and to consult with them about your argument. You might be favored by the wise, who often offer unexpected ideas.

When you speak, let even the foolish people know in advance the point about which you will speak. Then public opinion will tend to work to your advantage.

Or you might even talk to your servants or maid servants. Tell them something like this: "Since my opponent attacks in such a way, I will defend myself in such-and-such a manner." If you make such remarks repeatedly beforehand, then in the law court, you can develop your point smoothly and fluently. You will use the right words, and you will sound reasonable. But, if you keep your ideas to yourself and begin to discuss them without previous consultation and resolution, then you are sure to slip and make blunders.

At any rate, consultation is the key. If you cannot find a wise person, you'd better confer with your wife or children. While talking to them you might come to some spontaneous decision. Long experience alone makes you come across the appropriate idea or so Josui Mura told me.

You had better say all that you have to say at once because, if you bring up something later, it will sound like an excuse.

Also, you might remind your opponent of his statement and let him affirm the statement at intervals. In this manner, he cannot retract his remarks.

After convincing him of your point, if you instruct him further in useful information and lessons in his own self-interest, then your victory will become a greater victory.

This is a method consistent with propriety.

BOOK ELEVEN

Do Not Turn Your Back
on the Enemy

A samurai general said, "You need not test the back of the
armor worn by officers. Only test the front.

"No decorations on armor are necessary. But you must
examine and choose good helmets, which may eventually fall
into the enemy's hands with your heads."

Do Not Learn Strategy

Lord Shigekata once said, "There will be no learning strategy for my offspring. In the heat of the battle you cannot really suppress any sense of discretion you may have cultivated.
If you have discretion, you cannot break through the enemy.
It is important, therefore, in the time of 'before the month

of the tiger' (i.e., of war) that you be utterly indiscreet. With discretion you fall prey to suspicious misgivings and will have much difficulty in making a definite decision. Our offspring should not learn strategy."

Some Hints for Arguing

Some hints for arguing: first disarm your opponent by saying, "You are quite right." Then let your opponent speak fully. Wait for him to make a slip of the tongue. Then take advantage by catching him in his own words.

On Victory

One or two items in a verbatim note on swordsmanship: while having your skin cut, cut your opponent's bones. No indiscretion; then no victory.

How to Win in the Long Run

If you are promoted too quickly with a salary increase, every colleague, out of jealousy, will become your enemy. This is no good. If you rise too slowly then every colleague, out of pity, will become your friend. Then the many friends will guarantee your future success. After all, if no one is dissatisfied with your raise—whether quick or slow—then you are in no danger.

Good fortune that others want you to enjoy is your genuine and long-lived reward.

Success and Failure

It is said, "Small mistakes do not spoil a great accomplishment." As long as you dedicate yourself wholeheartedly to the Lord's service, it does not matter what you do outside of clan affairs. You can have your own way and do mischief if you must. On the other hand, those who are apparently faultless in every way often look very ugly. More often than not, they miss the important point. Only those who have made some mistakes can also accomplish great works. If you have great principles, your small faults can easily be justified.

Die Every Morning in Advance

The realization of certain death ought to be renewed every morning. Every morning you must prepare yourself for every kind of death. With composure of mind, think of yourself as shattered by bows, guns, spears, swords; as carried away by great billows of water; as running into a great fire; as struck by thunder and lightning; as shaken by severe earthquake; as diving from a cliff; as a disease-filled corpse; as an accidental death corpse.

An elder of the house said, "Once you go out from under the eaves, you are in the midst of death. Once you go out the gate, you come across enemies."

This is not mere precaution but the experiencing of death in advance.

To Be Taciturn

The highest achievement of talking is not to talk. If you decide to debate with no words, you may even find you can do without any speech. You had best speak no more than you have to. And say as few words as possible and in good order, too. It so often happens that you fall into disgrace when you speak recklessly and, by chance, reveal your shame.

Social Appearance

There are those who look bright at first sight. Even if they accomplish something big, people take it as a matter of course. And when they accomplish something others can do, then people will think of their accomplishment as unsatisfactory or less than expected. On the other hand, if those who look calm and meek should express themselves in little better than mediocre work, people will praise them for it.

A Story Concerning Family Honor

A samurai passed Hachinoe, a post-town in Saga (the capital of Hizen). Suddenly, he was attacked by diarrhea. He ran into a tenement-house on a side street and asked for a lavatory. As it happened, there was only a young wife in that house. She told him that the lavatory was at the back. Then he took off his *hakama* (trousers) and started for the toilet.

At that very moment, the husband returned home and accused them of adultery. Eventually the matter was brought before the court. The two were sentenced to death.

Lord Naoshige, hearing of this incident, judged as follows: "Even if this is not a case of a liaison, it is still the same. For not only did the samurai inadvertently take off his *hakama* in the presence of a young woman who was alone, but the woman also allowed him to take it off in the absence of her husband."

On Governing

It is very likely that people misunderstand that to govern the under-heaven (state) is a big problem and beyond their power.

The offices of the ministers at the Shogunate, and those of the Chief Retainers of the present clan, are no more difficult than I have explained here in this mountain hermitage. You can rule the whole nation on the basis of my talk.

I have some misgivings about our clansmen in office now. They have made no studies of our clan. They carry out their offices only as their natural, gifted ability dictates. So every subject who crawls under their authority (i.e., flatters them) is frightened and says "yes" all the time. Consequently the elders and superiors become obsessed with self-interest and self-conceit.

10 September
in the first year of Kyoho
(1716)

Footnotes

1. *Country* refers specifically to the ways and customs particular to the Nabeshima clan. In a general sense "country" refers to the clans that composed the individual states—today collectively known as Japan.

2. *Gochyu* (1454–1546) was the honorific name for Iekane Ryuzozi, who was one of the first founders of the Nabeshima clan.

3. *Riso* (1468–1552) was the honorific name for Kiyohisa Nabeshima, who was one of the first founders of the Nabeshima clan.

4. *Takanobu* (1529–1584) was one of the Ryuzozi family. He was also one of the first founders of the Nabeshima clan.

5. *Nippo* (1538–1618) was the honorific name for Naoshige Nabeshima, who was one of the first founders of the Nabeshima clan.

6. *Kusunoki* (1294–1336) was one of the best-known generals to fight in the cause of the emperor.

7. *Shingen* (1521–1336) was one of the best-known Lord-generals to fight in the cause of the emperor.

8. Each religion or philosophy, or belief or *Way*, has its own principal idol and image. Christianity has Christ; Buddhism has Buddha, etc.

9. *Harakiri* is an elaborate death ritual that culminates with the person thrusting a sword into his own stomach and disemboweling himself. Harakiri was the samurai's last resort to save face, because it was believed "if you are dead, no shame can come to you."

10. These two books were never published. They were considered the secret property of the Nabeshima family.

The phrase "at first hand" means passing directly from the Lord to his samurais.

11. *Chief Retainer* was the assistant and adviser of the Lord. Usually the Chief Retainer held the real power while the Lord was just a symbol. The office of Chief Retainer was hereditary.

12. *Ronin* is a "thrown-away" samurai: At some point in their training, samurais were asked to leave the Lord's household, either for punishment or for their own experience. The purpose was to have the samurai taste the miseries of life. During the ronin period, the samurai was considered masterless or lordless.

13. *Nirvana* is the summum bonum of Buddhism, the culmination of practice and enlightenment. Literally, it is the end of conditioned living and its suffering.

Glossary

Bon. A Lantern Festival during which the souls of the ancestors are worshipped. Also called the *Bon Matsuri* or *Urabon*, this is one of the most popular annual festivals in Japan. The Bon has both Buddhist and Shinto origins.

Bonze. A Buddhist monk.

Calligraphy. The art of fine handwriting.

Chanoyo. *See* Tea ceremony.

Chief Retainer. The assistant to and adviser of the Lord. Usually, the Chief Retainer holds the real power while the Lord is just a symbol. The office of Chief Retainer is hereditary.

Coward. One who shows fear when faced with pain or danger. The worst curse for a samurai is to be called a coward. This means that he is anything but a samurai. It implies that he lacks the samurai spirit and fails to meet the standards of Bushido. For a samurai, "coward" denotes both social disgrace and inner failure.

Dharuma. A tumbler doll. The term *dharuma* originates with Bodhidharma, the Indian Brahmin, who brought Zen Buddhism from India to China in the sixth century, and became the first Chinese Patriarch.

Esprit de corps. A shared spirit of comradeship and devotion to a cause among the members of a group.

Geisha. One of a professional class of women in Japan whose occupation is to entertain men through singing, dancing, and providing social companionship. A geisha is used like a tool, in contrast to the samurai, who is a tool plus the whole self which is the executive samurai. The geisha takes her art of entertaining very seriously; yet for the samurai, the geisha is merely a plaything that can amuse him. The samurai plays many games, but he does not take them seriously.

Ghost. The spirit of a dead person. The implication is that even as a ghost or spirit, you can protect your Lord. You don't necessarily need your body form to do him service.

Gongen. A war god, believed by the Japanese to be a manifestation of Buddha.

Harakiri. An elaborate ritual suicide in which the samurai thrusts a sword into his own stomach and disembowels himself. Harakiri is the samurai's last resort to save face.

Inka. A certificate awarded to one who has experienced Enlightment (*satori*).

Kamigata. A calculating Bushido who prefers life to death, considered by the author to be inferior to the Bushido associated with Zen Buddhism, which teaches transcendence of the dichotomy of life and death.

Kenko Yoshida. A Buddhist monk poet and essayist (1282–1350).

Koan. In Japanese Zen Buddhism, a short paradoxical question or statement used for meditation by novices. One of the best-known koans is, "What is the sound of one hand clapping?" When two hands clap, a sound is heard, but the monk is asked to reflect on the sound made by one hand (equivalent to his true self or Buddha-Nature).

Light-legged. Samurais of the lowest rank, so-called because they wear light armor in a battle.

Maboroshi. A vision or a dreamlike state.

Nirvana. In Buddhism, the ultimate state that can be attained, characterized by wisdom, compassion, composure, and sympathetic joy. As the culmination of practice and enlightenment, Nirvana is the end of all suffering.

Ronin. A "thrown-away" samurai who is asked to leave the Lord's household, either for punishment or for experience, so that the samurai will taste the miseries of life. During the ronin period, the samurai is considered masterless and lordless.

Saigyo. A Buddhist monk poet (1118–1190).

Satori. In Japanese Zen Buddhism, the inner experience of enlightenment. (*Satori* in Japanese means "to realize.")

Sumo. A style of Japanese wrestling in which size, weight, and strength are of most importance. The sumo ring is circular in shape. The general rule of the game is that if a wrestler either falls off his feet or is pushed out of the circle, he loses.

Tea ceremony. Called *chanoyo* in Japanese, the ancient ritual of preparing, serving, and drinking tea. The tea ceremony is founded upon the adoration of the beautiful in daily life.

Torii. The gateway marking the entrance of a Shinto temple. Characteristically, it consists of two cylindrical vertical posts topped by two crosswise rectangular beams, one of which is positioned slightly lower than the other.

Index

THE BUDDHA'S GOLDEN PATH

The Classic Introduction to Zen Buddhism

Dwight Goddard

In 1929, when author Dwight Goddard wrote *The Buddha's Golden Path,* he was breaking ground. No American before him had lived the lifestyle of a Zen Buddhist monk, and then set out to share the secrets he had learned with his countrymen. This title was the first American book published to popularize Zen Buddhism. Released in the midst of the Great Depression, in its own way, it offered answers to the questions that millions of disillusioned people were beginning to ask—questions about what was really important in their lives. Questions we still ask ourselves today.

As a book of instruction, *The Buddha's Golden Path* has held up remarkably well. As a true classic, it has touched countless lives, and has opened the door for future generations in this country to study and embrace the principles of Zen.

$14.95 • 208 pages • 5.5 x 8.5-inch quality paperback • 2-color • Religion/Zen Buddhism • ISBN 0-7570-0023-1

I CHING FOR A NEW AGE

The Book of Answers for Changing Times

Edited by Robert G. Benson

For over three thousand years, the Chinese have placed great value on the *I Ching*—also called the "Classic of Changes" and the "Book of Changes"—turning to it for guidance and insight. The *I Ching* is based on the deep understanding that our lives go through definable patterns, which can be determined by "consulting the Oracle"—the book of *I Ching.* Throughout the centuries, *I Ching* devotees have used the book as a means of understanding past, present, and future events, as well as exercising control over some events. The book highlights hundreds of different possibilities we might face in daily life, both on a professional and on a personal level.

For over ten years, researcher Robert Benson worked towards making the English text of the *I Ching* easier to understand and use. The result is a book that focuses on the text's essential meaning and is highly accessible to the modern Western reader. In addition, Benson provides an illuminating history of the *I Ching,* explaining how the text was created, discussing how it works, and exploring its many mysteries. Here is an *I Ching* that stands alone, providing a book of answers for anyone who faces a time of personal crisis and change.

$17.95 • 352 pages • 5.5 x 8.5-inch quality paperback • 2-color • Spiritualism/Chinese • ISBN 0-7570-0019-3

The Wit and Wisdom of the Talmud

Proverbs, Sayings, and Parables for the Ages

Edited by George J. Lankevich

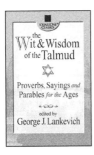

In Jewish tradition, the Talmud embodies the laws of Judaism, as well as a way of study and intellectual development. Composed of two works, the Mishnah and the Gemara, the Talmud is believed to provide serious students with one of the most sacred of experiences. It is, in fact, the Torah—the Old Testament—and the Talmud that offer the tenets of the Jewish religion.

Here, in this classic work—representing almost two thousand years of learning—are those pearls of wisdom that we can all benefit from and enjoy time and time again. Some may be familiar to you; others may be new. All, however, can offer illuminating insights and direction throughout your life.

$13.95 • 176 pages • 5.5 x 8.5-inch quality paperback • 2-color • Religion/Judaism/Talmud • ISBN 0-7570-0021-5

Tao Te Ching
The Way of Virtue

Lao Tzu • Translated by Patrick Michael Byrne

The *Tao Te Ching* has served as a personal road map for millions of people. It is said that its words reveal the underlying principles that govern the world in which we live. Holding to the laws of nature—drawing from the essence of what all things are—it offers both a moral compass and an internal balance. A fundamental book of the Taoist, the *Tao Te Ching* is regarded as a revelation in its own right. For those seeking a better understanding of themselves, it provides a wealth of wisdom and insights.

Through time—from one powerful dynasty to another—many changes have been made to the original Chinese text of the *Tao Te Ching*. Over the last century, translators have added to the mix by incorporating their interpretations. While jackhammering its original text, some have created beautiful versions of the *Tao Te Ching* in the name of poetic license. Others have relied on variant forms of the original, while still others have added their own philosophical spins to the material. For those readers who are looking for a purer interpretation of the *Tao Te Ching*, researcher Patrick Michael Byrne has produced a translation that is extremely accurate, while capturing the pattern and harmony of the original. Here is a *Tao Te Ching* that you can enjoy, understand, and value.

$14.95 • 176 pages • 5.5 x 8.5-inch quality paperback • 2-color • Spiritualism/Chinese • ISBN 0-7570-0029-0

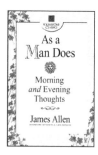

As a Man Does
Morning and Evening Thoughts
James Allen

One of the first great modern writers of motivational and inspirational books, James Allen has influenced millions of people around the world through books like *As a Man Thinketh*. In the same way, *As a Man Does: Morning and Evening Thoughts* presents beautiful and insightful meditations to feed the mind and soul.

In each of the sixty-two meditations—one for each morning and each evening of the month—Allen offers both the force of truth and the blessing of comfort. Whether you are familiar with the writings of James Allen or you have yet to read any of his stirring books, this beautiful volume is sure to move you, console you, and inspire you—every morning and every evening of your life.

$8.95 • 96 pages • 5.5 x 8.5-inch quality paperback • 2-color • Inspiration/Religion • ISBN 0-7570-0018-5

The New Revelation
My Personal Investigation of Spiritualism
Sir Arthur Conan Doyle

The spiritual movement in the early part of the twentieth century had few proponents greater than Sir Arthur Conan Doyle—a medical doctor, soldier, intellect, and world-renowned author of the Sherlock Holmes series. In 1918, Doyle published *The New Revelation*—a firsthand account of his personal investigation into the world of Spiritualism, which embraced areas that we refer to today as ESP, New Age philosophy, metaphysics, and psychic experiences. While some may view this work as a historical footnote, the answers to Sir Arthur's basic questions about life and death are as relevant today as they were then.

An original Introduction to the book provides an insightful look at Doyle's personal life, and his friendship with magician Harry Houdini is brilliantly captured in an original Afterword.

$12.95 • 148 pages • 5.5 x 8.5-inch quality paperback • 2-color • Inspiration/Religion • ISBN 0-7570-0017-7